Imprint

© 2019 Caroline Zierold
Publisher : Caroline Zierold, Munich, Germany

ISBN: 9781674675619

Print: Amazon Media EU S.à r.l. (Société à responsabilité limitée), 38 avenue John F. Kennedy, L-1855 Luxembourg

Layout and Cover: Caroline Zierold

Bibliographic information of the German National Library:

The Deutsche Nationalbibliothek lists this publication in the Deutsche Nationalbibliografie; detailed bibliographic data can be found on the Internet at *http://dnb.dnb.de.*

Te Araroa Trail

The ultimate guide for the Te Araroa Trail in New Zealand

Caroline Zierold

Contents

Let's go

Hello, my name is Caro. I'm 30 years old, a product designer, come from Munich and love nature, especially hiking. During my studies, I traveled through South America and lived in Spain. As I'd been doing day hikes for quite a few years, I felt the need for a new challenge. I decided I wanted to hike a longer distance that would take several days. So, in the summer of 2014, I hiked the GR 11, an 820 km long distance hike through the Pyrenees, from the Atlantic coast to the Mediterranean. At the time, the GR 11 was perfect for getting a taste of long-distance hiking.

After I completed my Bachelor's degree in 2016, I traveled to Canada for a year and guided sled dog tours, but I really wanted to hike a longer trail again. I had always been interested in visiting New Zealand, so I searched for „long distance trail in New Zealand" on the Internet. I came across the Te Araroa Trail, and decided to give it a try!

Why did I write a guide for the Te Araroa Trail?

I decided to write this guide because I had a lot of questions before I started the trail, and it took me quite a long time to collect all the important information. I would have saved a lot of time, effort, and stress if I had more Trail Insider info. That's why I've packed all the important information into this book. With this guide, you can prepare for the trail and get an idea about what to expect on the Te Araroa Trail.

All websites and links mentioned in this guide can be found online. Simply type them into your browser.

A short note: It's always a bit different to walk solo as a woman. Therefore, there is a separate section for solo hikers/women on selected topics.

Have fun reading, Caro

If you have suggestions for the guidebook or further questions about the trail, you are also welcome to contact me personally at
carozierold@gmail.com or via my website: www.teararoaguide.de

What was my motivation to walk the Te Araroa trail?

A very good question, which I occasionally asked myself during my time on the TA (Te Araroa Trail). I'm pretty sure that everyone has their own personal motivation and reasons for doing such a long hike.

My goal was to master a trail longer than the GR 11 and, above all, to explore a country in a different way. I also wanted to know if my body would carry me 3,000 kilometers through New Zealand. You'll be amazed at how quickly the body adapts to new challenges.

While the Te Araroa Trail is definitely a challenge, anyone who can walk normally can do it! You don't need alpine mountaineering experience or climbing experience, and navigation on the trail with maps and/or mobile phone is no problem at all.

Why New Zealand?

On the TA, you hike through every kind of landscape you can imagine! New Zealand is stunningly unique, and during your hike you will see rain forests, turquoise sea, natural beaches, crystal clear rivers, and beautiful mountain scenes. It's unrivaled beauty makes this trail worth the effort!!

But, of course, the trail is also a challenge.

You will walk on roads and highways (especially on the North Island), cross rivers, trudge in the sand and mud, walk in the pouring rain, in blazing heat. You'll hike countless vertical meters up and down...but, as I said, it's worth it! Even though there were many difficult situations on the trail, in the end, I was proud of my accomplishment.

Apart from nature, you won't believe how nice and helpful the locals (Kiwis) are. I was often offered food, cold drinks, or even a lift by car to resupply my food. On top of that, I even camped overnight for free in a local's garden. It didn't really matter if I was hiking on my own or in a small group, people just wanted to support and help. Of course, you'll also meet very nice and friendly TA Hikers on the Trail. For me this was an important part of the trail, because some of the people I hiked with became very good friends.

The Te Araroa Trail

What is the Te Araroa Trail, and why should I donate?

The Te Araroa Trail is a 3,000 km long trail from Cape Reinga to Bluff. The trail officially opened on 3 December, 2011 and is called "New Zealand's Trail." Funnily enough, many Kiwis have never heard of the trail. The so-called Te Araroa Trust, which takes care of all aspects of the trail (maintenance, trail notes, maps, permits, etc.), is completely financed by donations, private sponsors, and volunteer work. For this reason, a donation of $250 per island is suggested. You can donate online at *https://www.teararoa.org.nz/donate/*

Website and Facebook Group

Check the official Te Araroa website at *https://www.teararoa.org.nz/* for downloads, trail updates, and additional information.

Also, consider joining one of the Te Araroa Facebook groups. Just search for *Te Araroa* on Facebook and join the group.

Trail - How, Where, When?

In general, it's always a good idea to tell someone responsible your trip intentions. Let them know in detail where you're going, time and date when you leave for the hike, when you plan to return, and who is going with you for each section of the hike. Don't forget to let your contact know when you've completed a section of the trail. It is also important to check the weather regularly, have the right equipment and enough food with you at all times.

How do I walk the trail? Can I skip sections?

Everyone walks the trail in their own way; you'll meet everyone from the „Purist" (hiker who walks every meter), to the „80 km per day hiker," and the „As slow as possible hiker. You can combine the trail as you want, (e.g., hitchhike the highways and walk all the hiking trails). Also keep in mind, that the trail is not a race, the experience is what counts in the end.

How well is the Trail developed and marked?

The TA is quite well-developed and marked. You follow orange triangles which show you where to go. You rarely walk without markings, but even in these places, the direction is clear. If you should lose your way, you can use topographical maps, trail notes, or the Guthook app (see the Navigation chapter for details). Even if you should get lost, you will be able to find your way back on the trail.

However, you can't compare hiking in New Zealand to hiking in Europe. New Zealand trails are more strenuous and less well-developed. Walking through rough terrain and river crossings are an integral part of the so-called tramping in New Zealand.

Here, you get an overview of what the different trail markings look like. As already mentioned above, you almost always follow orange triangles.

Trail marker on a tree

Trail marker in tussock

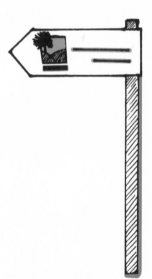

Trail marker on roads

Trail marker on pasture

Notes:

When's the best time to Start?

TA Southbound

The best months to start TA Southbound are between mid-September and early January. Most people start the trail in the first weeks of October, so if you want to do a little more hiking by yourself, I would start in mid-September (Note: it can still be a bit cold and rainy). In addition, some parts of the trail are still closed this early in the season. Information about the trail status can be found on the official Te Araroa website:

https://www.teararoa.org.nz/trailstatus/

If you want to meet other hikers and are open to hiking with a larger group, I would start in Cape Reinga in October. This way, you will meet many other TA hikers early on in your journey.

TA Northbound

If you want to do the Trail Northbound and start in Bluff, the best months are between November and January. I wouldn't start Northbound earlier than the beginning of December because there might still be snow in the mountains. Also, the chances are relatively high that it will snow and become very cold from mid April on the South Island.

The official Te Araroa website says:" If you don't feel very comfortable walking in the rain and cold, you should start Southbound between the end of October and the beginning of November and Northbound between the end of December and the beginning of January". However, the weather in New Zealand is unpredictable; it can even snow in high summer (South Island). For this reason, it is good to stick roughly to the suggestions. Of course it is not recommended to do the trail completely in the New Zealand winter, i.e. June to August.

Southbound Start: October - November
Northbound Start: December - January

Should I walk Southbound or Northbound?

Southbound Pros

- The trail notes are very detailed with good descriptions (North + South Island).
- You will meet many other TA hikers if you start in the high season from the beginning of October until the beginning of November.
- The North Island prepares you well for the South Island you'll be physically and mentally prepared for the more difficult conditions of the South Island.
- Whanganui River with a canoe. This stretch is only possible downstream, so heading south means you don't have to take a detour.

Southbound Cons

- The trail can be a bit overcrowded. I hiked with a maximum of 7 other people, and if you like, you can always walk alone.
- The huts can get quite crowded from time to time.

Northbound Pros

- You will be on your own a lot, as most hikers walk the TA Southbound instead of Northbound.
- You did the South Island first, which means the North Island will be super easy for you (less altitude difference).

Northbound Cons

- There are no official Trail notes for the North Island, only for the South Island, and these are not as detailed as the Southbound Trail notes.
- If you want to canoe the Whanganui River, you have to travel (probably hitch hike) from Wanganui to Taumarunui or Ohakune. From there you can organize and plan the canoe trip.

How much time do I need for the complete trail?

It is said that 50 to 80 days are needed per island (without rest days). Therefore, you need between 3.3 and 5.3 months for the complete trail. But the total length of the trail depends on how many kilometers you walk per day and how many rest days you take. In addition, the weather may cause delays.

I needed 60 days for the North Island. I never walked more than 40 kilometers a day, and more precisely, I only had two 40-kilometer days. On all other days, I hiked between 20 and 35 kilometers. For the South Island, it took me almost 2.5 months, which is pretty long. Sometimes, the weather didn't cooperate, and I had to wait it out because either the rivers were too high or it snowed in the mountains. I walked a total of 4.5 months (with rest days).

Plan on a generous time window of 6 months, then you can be 100% sure to be able you will walk the whole trail. This way you have no time pressure, you can take a rest day every now and then, and you can also do side-trips. If you don't plan side trips during your hike, you'll still have time after the trail to visit other nice places in New Zealand.

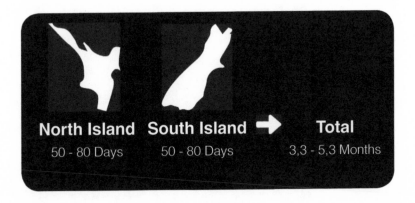

North Island   **South Island** ➡   **Total**
50 - 80 Days   50 - 80 Days   3,3 - 5,3 Months

Walking solo or in a group?

That depends on you, but, of course, everyone can start the trail alone. If you start during the high season, you will probably meet other TA Hikers within the first few days. In general you don't have to worry about walking alone for extended periods of time, but if you want, you can.

I walked the trail partly in a larger group, but mostly in a group of two. If you prefer to be alone, I would either go Northbound or start the trail relatively early/late in the season.

Solo Hiking

As a solo hiker, you are very safe in New Zealand. The people are friendly and helpful. It is unlikely that you would find yourself in a dangerous or unpleasant situation.

It helps to consider which situations would make you feel unsafe. For example, you may feel uncomfortable if you know that you have to sleep somewhere alone on the trail. To avoid this, you could group together with other hikers during the day. You will always find enough people to feel safe if you start in the high season and walk Southbound.

Additionally, you don't have to worry about poisonous or dangerous animals because they don't exist in New Zealand!

Notes:

Documents

Visa for New Zealand

If you want to go to New Zealand, you have to apply for a visa before entering the country. There most common visas include:

Visitor Visa

https://www.immigration.govt.nz/new-zealand-visas/apply-for-a-visa/about-visa/visitor-visa

Work and Holiday Visa

https://www.immigration.govt.nz/new-zealand-visas/options/work/thinking-about-coming-to-new-zealand-to-work/working-holiday-visa

Flights

Booking the flight as early as possible is always cheaper than buying the tickets last minute.

Travel Health Insurance

You must have health insurance if you want to enter New Zealand with a Work and/or Holiday/Visitor Visa. Simply print out the confirmation as proof that you're covered.

Bank Account and Credit Card Account

A credit card will allow you to get money abroad or withdraw funds with in New Zealand. If you come to New Zealand on a Work and Holiday Visa, you can also open a New Zealand bank account.

To transfer money to your New Zealand account, you can simply use Transferwise. The currency conversion is always up to date and you pay a minimum amount of fees for the transfer itself. More information can be found at *https://transferwise.com*

Weather

You'll find all types of weather in New Zealand. It might experience snow, rain, sweltering, and stormy all in one day. The weather is quite unpredictable because New Zealand's two islands are not protected by any neighboring mainland. Therefore, you should check the weather forecast regularly to prepare for bad weather. In addition, you should have the right equipment for any kind of weather. It is also advisable to take an extra daily ration of food. This could be helpful if you should have to wait out bad weather.

You can get a good weather forecast on *www.yr.no* and *https://www.metservice.com/national/home*.
Metservice provides a good app as well.

Sun Protection

You should always have sun cream with you because the sun in New Zealand is extremely strong. For example, I always walked in long clothes, with leggings and long sleeves. This worked well for me, even on hot days because I was always protected from the sun, and I only had to apply sun cream to my face and hands.

Sand Flies

In New Zealand, you'll encounter sand flies, which are small flies that bite. The bites are quite itchy. Long clothing helps to prevent sand fly bites, and tea tree oil alleviates the itching without the use of chemicals.

Current Route Conditions: DOC and i-Sites

DOC

DOC is the Department of Conservation. They are responsible for the maintenance of almost all hiking trails and huts in New Zealand. Information from the DOC can be found all over New Zealand. DOC trail signs are green with yellow lettering and are found all over the TA trail. In larger cities the DOC has DOC Visitor Centres where you can get information about hiking trails and the weather forecast. The staff members are usually rangers, which means they can give you competent information about the trail and the weather.

I - Sites (Information Centres)

I-site is New Zealand's official visitor information network. There are 80 I-sites throughout the country. You can also get information and updates about the weather in the mountains. If you should decide to leave the trail for a side trip, the I-sites provide you with good ideas and information.

Notes:

Hut Pass and Permits

Hut Pass

A hut pass allows you to sleep in DOC huts during your hike. On the South Island it is cheaper to buy a DOC hut pass, rather than pay for lodging every single night. You can buy the pass at the DOC visitor center or at the iSites in almost every city in New Zealand.

The price is:

- 9 months ($92)
- 12 months ($122)

Where can I buy the pass?

Southbound - Start North Island	**Auckland**
Southbound - Start South Island	**Wellington**

Northbound - Start North Island	**Wellington**
Northbound - Start South Island	**Invercargill**

If you don't want to get your pass at one of these places, the following website gives information where else you can buy a season pass.

https://www.doc.govt.nz/hutticketretailers

Without a hut pass, you have to buy a single ticket for each hut. This is complicated and much more expensive than the hut pass. This method is only practical if you are hiking just the North Island.

Permits (approval)

For the Queen Charlotte Track (far north of the South Island), you need an extra permit. Check out where you can buy the permit at *www.qctlc.com/ testimonials.html*

Where to sleep?

The Huts

On the TA you'll see pretty much every kind and size of DOC huts. These cabins are equipped with mattresses for sleeping, drinking water (water tank), cooking facilities (sink plus running water, no hot plates, no gas) and almost always with an oven (sometimes, you can cook on the oven). However, there are no outlets to charge mobile phones, power banks, etc.

There are also hut books in every hut. You should always enter your complete name, date, direction (where you are heading to), and the number of your hut pass in each of these books because it may assist in search and rescue operations in case of emergency.

There are also a few huts where you'll come across mice. To make sure your food doesn't get eaten, it's handy to have all your food in a dry bag and hang it up.
Occasionally, during my trip, the huts were a bit crowded. On those nights, I preferred to sleep in my tent, because I don't like it at all when someone snores. But most of the time I could sleep in the huts without any problems - sometimes even by myself.

For Women

It is also best to take tampons and sanitary pads out of your backpack overnight. Mice like to crawl into backpacks and use these items to make their nests nice and cozy. No kidding :)

Camping

North Island - On the North Island, you can spend almost every night at campsites, also called Holiday Parks. This costs between 17 and 20 dollars per person in a tent. The campgrounds are normally equipped with hot showers, kitchen, water, electricity, TV lounge, WiFi (limited), washrooms and dryers (4 dollars per wash, 4 dollars per dry). Sometimes, locals also offer private campsites (especially on the North Island section). You will usually find a sign saying „Camping," an Honesty Box to deposit your cash, a good area to pitch your tent, drinking water and toilets. Sometimes, you have to call the owners and pay them personally. Details can be found in the trailnotes.

South Island – You rarely have to camp on the South Island, as you can sleep almost every night in one of the DOC huts. But be sure to take a tent with you because the huts may be full. Apart from that, a tent allows flexibility as you decide where to sleep on the trail.

DOC campgrounds

On the TA, you will also find campgrounds that are maintained and managed by DOC. These are much simpler than the Holiday Park campsites and cost between 8 and 13 dollars per person/per night. You deposit cash into an „Honesty Box," so it is always good to have some money with you. Often, the campgrounds are located on large meadows, where you can find plenty of space to pitch your tent. There are always toilets and often picnic tables. Sometimes, the campgrounds offer shelters where you can cook, eat, and be protected from wind and rain. In addition, there is drinking water at every DOC campground. In general there are not outlets to charge your mobile phone.

In New Zealand, you don't have to make a reservation for a campsite because the sites, Holiday Parks or DOC, are rarely full.

Tip! It is always worth asking for a TA discount at Holiday Parks. Sometimes, you get up to 10 dollars discount.

Camping in the Wild

I wild camped much more on the North- than on the South- Island as there are a lot of nice DOC huts to stay.

If you want to wild camp, there are a few simple rules. Please don't leave any garbage, so always take plastic bags, etc. with you. To "do your business," you should dig a hole and bury any solid waste, including toilet paper. In addition, always stay 50 to 100 meters away from rivers and streams. Do not bury tampons, sanitary pads and baby wipes. Please take them with you and dispose them at the next opportunity. You should also use water sparingly and do not pour chemicals into the water. Always use chemical-free soap for washing which you can buy in almost every outdoor shop in NZ (e.g. *Dr. Bronner's soap*).

Sleep in a Local's Garden

Sometimes it's a bit tricky to find a suitable camp spot, so it can be handy to ask locals if you are allowed to pitch your tent in their garden. That may sound strange, but many TA hikers do so. Kiwis are so friendly that you usually get a „yes" as an answer. Sometimes they offer you a beer on top of that! Unbelievable but true!! However, staying in a local's garden is a privilege and should not be taken for granted.

Hostels/Hotels

Occasionally you´ll have the option to sleep in a hostel/hotel. More information can be found in the TA Trailnotes or on the Guthook App. As with campsites, it's always worth asking for a TA discount.

Notes:

Navigation

Maps

If you should decide to walk with topo maps, you can download the complete trail maps here: *https://www.teararoa.org.nz/downloads/*.

It's better not to print all the maps at once because that's several hundred pages of paper, which makes your backpack unnecessarily heavy. Also make sure to have a waterproof map case. The easiest way to carry your maps is to print the maps for each section of the trail one at a time. For instance, if you walk Southbound and start with the North Island, I'd print the North Island section first, which is already 22 pages. In order to print out more map material, it is practical to have all files on a USB stick or a memory card so you can simply print out the maps once you need them. You can print the topo maps in libraries (there are a lot of them in New Zealand, and you'll pass quite a few). To save paper, print on both sides. To use the topographic maps correctly, you should have a compass with you and know how to use a map and compass together.

Trail Notes

The trail notes describe the complete Te Araroa Trail and are incredibly helpful. They help you know what to expect next on the trail regarding terrain, river crossings, elevation gain, huts, campgrounds, etc., and they clearly describe each part of the trail.

You can either print out the notes or download them to your mobile phone. I downloaded the trail notes as a PDF on my phone, which worked well, and I didn't have to carry any paper with me.

The download is available at *https://www.teararoa.org.nz/downloads/*

Bellow is an example of what trail notes look like:

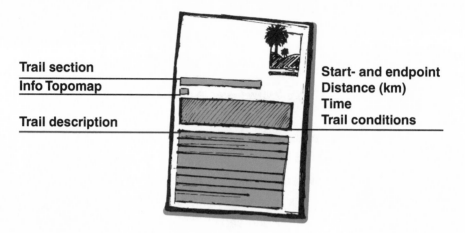

Guthook App

Guthook is an offline GPS app for hikers. It allows you to see your exact position on the trail. In addition, you get information about water sources, accommodation (hotels, hostels, campgrounds, huts, etc.), mountain peaks, and many other useful things for the trail. You can also check the number of kilometers you have completed. An elevation profile gives you a nice overview of what to expect and how much more there is to climb. The app is very helpful, and it makes the trail easier, especially during sections which are less well marked. You can also adjust the Guthook App for Southbound or Northbound hiking.

The complete TA package costs 40 USD. If you plan to hike only part of the TA, the North + South Island are divided into two sections; each section costs 13 USD, for a total of 26 USD per island. You can simply download the Guthook app to your mobile phone and buy the TA package/parts separately. The app works on Apple and Android phones.

Notes:

PLB - Personal locator beacon

What is a PLB?

A Personal Locator Beacon (PLB) is a small GPS device that can be activated in an emergency situation to alert the search and rescue authorities that you or someone else needs help. If you activate the beacon, the Rescue Coordination Centre New Zealand (RCCNZ) will get the exact coordinates of the activated PLB and then try to send help as quickly as possible.

Why Should I get a PLB?

In New Zealand, you rarely have cell phone reception outside of cities, so it is advisable to take a PLB with you. In addition, the trails are not as well-developed as in Europe. You'll also walk through very remote areas. Everyone who hikes the TA should definitely use a PLB because they can save your life in an emergency situation. Personally, I would never go without! Even if you are travelling in pairs or with several people, you should carry a PLB with you. If you are traveling in a group, you should have several PLBs.

Where Can I get a PLB?

You can get Personal Locator Beacons in New Zealand at any major outdoor store, including Kathmandu, MacPac, Bivouac and Hunting and Fishing. If you're looking for a more affordable option, I recommend asking via post in the Te Araroa FB group. Quite often people sell their PLBs after finishing the trail.

Register the PLB

To use the PLB, you must first register it online in New Zealand. Registration is free and easy. On the registration website you will be able to give information about yourself and your emergency contacts. If you should get into an emergency situation the RCCNZ can notify your contacts.

https://beacons.org.nz/Registration.aspx

Where Do I Carry the PLB?

The PLB should always be worn where it is easily accessible, ideally on your body. I always had my PLB attached to the shoulder straps of my rucksack. If there's a possibility of being separated from your backpack, it's recommended carrying the PLB on your body (e.g. at river crossings).

If you want to find out more information about a PLB, have a look at this website:

https://www.maritimenz.govt.nz/recreational/safety/communications/beacons/

A very good article about the importance of carrying a PLB can be found here:

https://wilderlife.nz/2019/05/where-and-how-do-you-carry-your-plb/

Notes:

Mobile Phone

Mobile Providers

The four most popular mobile operators in New Zealand are:

Spark

Spark has pink/white phone boxes, which are wifi zones, in almost every city in New Zealand. At these boxes you can use 1 GB per day for free. You will need a prepaid contract which costs $19 per month to use the wifi.
https://www.spark.co.nz/

Vodafone

https://www.vodafone.co.nz/

Skinny

With Skinny you normally have rollover data, which means, if you don't use your data in a certain month, it will be transferred to the next one. There's a Skinny app as well where you can check how much data, free minutes, etc. you have already used.
https://www.skinny.co.nz/pricing/plans/

2 Degrees

https://www.2degreesmobile.co.nz/

Mobile Phone Reception

There is cell phone reception in every city as well as in small villages. In general, you will have mobile phone reception more often on the North Island than the South Island because the trail sections on the South Island are longer and more remote. Every now and then it is worth checking your phone because you do have some cell phone coverage on some parts of the TA (e.g.Richmond Ranges, Timber Trail).

Tips for using the phone on the trail

Of course, you can use your phone to listen to music/podcasts, check the GPS and trail notes, and to take photos. To make sure that you still have enough battery, you should either do this during a shorter trail section or when you're sure to be able to charge your phone soon. Podcasts and music are great, especially on flat and less scenic parts of the trail; you'll see time flies by.

Tips for saving battery

- Put the phone in flight mode, as it will use hardly any battery.
- Reduce display brightness.
- Put your phone to battery-saving mode.
- Don't leave the GPS activated in the Guthook App. Only turn it on once you open the app. Don't forget to switch off the GPS again, otherwise the phone will die quickly.
- Switch off your mobile phone overnight.

Recharging the phone on the trail

Quite a few sections of the TA will take several days of hiking, which means you'll have to charge your phone at least once. It's best to take a powerbank with you. For most hikers this should be enough to charge your phone two times. Just keep in mind that you always want to carry as little weight as possible.

Feel free to check out the following website to see how many times your power bank can charge your phone.

https://www.aukey.com/battery-charge-calculator

As an alternative, you could use a solar panel. But these generally take longer to charge, are quite heavy, and if there´s no sunlight it won't work well.

Tips For Free Wifi in New Zealand

There´s good WiFi in libraries, at the McDonald's and Burger King, and in almost all cafes in NZ. You will also be able to use wifi in hostels, campgrounds, and iSite buildings.

Food

Cold or warm food?

The first question you'll probably ask yourself is whether you want to cook or just eat cold food. If you don't want to cook, you'll be able to save the weight of cooking equipment as well as the gas cartridge. Luckily there are plenty of lightweight cooking gear available. Also, if you ever need to replace your cooking equipment, New Zealand has a good variety in the outdoor shops.

I personally find cooking with camping gas out of a cartridge most suitable for long distance hikes. Using petrol is, in my opinion, rather impractical because its too heavy. New Zealand outdoor shops usually offer camping gas which is suitable for an attachment with screw valve. I was using the *Msr PocketRocket 2* stove and it fit on every gas cartridge.
https://www.msrgear.com/ie/stoves/canister-stoves/pocketro-cket-2-stove/09884.html?srd=true

What should I consider?

Basically, you should choose foods rich in nutrients, high in carbs, and tasty! Every long distance hiker dreams about super light, fresh food that has a tiny pack size. But it's not always easy to find a good balance between weight, size and good nutrition. Generally speaking, it's good to try to eat as balanced as possible. Especially if you have to walk a long section (several days) this can be tricky because healthy, fresh food typically weighs a lot.

In general, the topic of food is very important on a long-distance hike. After only a few days you'll probably start to fantasize about fresh salad, ice cream or a fat burger. Therefore it is good to put some money aside for such things (ice cream, coffee, and chips cost around 4 to 5 NZ dollars each).

Personally, I always felt that I wanted to eat unhealthy, fatty foods first and then something healthy. You should also fill up on vitamins with fresh fruits and veggies regularly; it's easy to do so during resupplying. Also, if the section wasn't too long, I usually took some fresh fruits with me. My backpack was heavier, but I was able to eat fresh food for a bit longer.

What can I get at the Supermarket in New Zealand?

You get every kind of food; NZ supermarkets are well stocked. But be aware that New Zealand is very expensive. A pepper costs around 5 NZ dollars, an avocado 6 NZ dollars (depending on the season).

Which supermarkets are in New Zealand?

Pak´n Save – cheapest, largest selection.
New World and Countdown - most frequently seen, a good product range.
Fresh Choice – good product range.
Four square - mostly smaller and more expensive, smaller variety of food.

To give you some inspiration, on the next page, you will find a list with an overview of my trail food for one complete day. This is just an example. Sometimes there are several options mentioned.

Breakfast

Porridge with cinamon and sugar (with milk/almond powder or water), JED´s coffee (pre-packed coffee in tea bags).

Lunch

- **Example 1:** Nuts (Almonds, cashews, peanuts) mixed with raisins and cranberries (one full Ziploc bag), 2 granola bars (two regular ones or one OSM bar)
- **Example 2:** One or two wraps with peanut butter, cheese and raisins etc.

Dinner

- **Example 1:** instant mashed potatoes with butter and croutons
- **Example 2:** Couscous with spices
- **Example 3:** Pasta (2 minute spaghetti) with tomato paste and cheese

For dessert chocolate (Whittakers is the best one!)

Food Hacks

- OSM bars. These are more expensive than normal cereal bars, but they are less sugary and very filling so they almost replace a complete meal.Uncooked instant noodles work well as a snack. This sounds weird, but they actually taste good!

- Add spices to everything you might eat "plain," for example couscous. This will make your experience much more enjoyable.

- Pre-pack and ration everything! Pack each meal separately. Put e.g. couscous in small Ziploc bags and add the spices, etc. into each bag so you have all the ingredients ready for cooking.

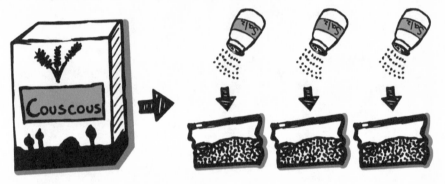

- Overnight Oats - You can soak your oatmeal overnight. Saves time in the mornings.

- You can get fresh coffee in tea bags, the brand is called JED'S, it's so tasty.

- Rice, lentils, beans etc. can be soaked in water during the day (e.g. empty peanut butter jar) This reduces cooking time and use of camping gas.

-
-

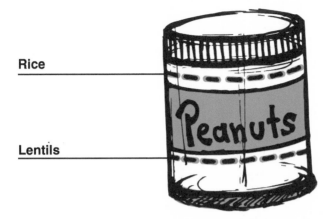

Rice

Lentils

- To get even more protein, you can also pack protein powder into portions and drink it during the day. There are also vegan options available.

- For those who aren't vegetarian/vegan, you can get tuna in sachets, which are much lighter than the canned tuna and are a good source of protein.

- Backcountrymeal - These are dehydrated meals that only requires hot water to prepare. You can get them in every supermarket. I would recommend the two-person portion. A backcountry meal costs between 8 and 12 dollars, which is quite expensive in the long run.

- Reuse Ziploc bags several times because of all the plastic garbage that already exists.

- Sometimes, you can get food and even camping gas for free. Always check the free box at campsites and hostels.

How to pack my food?

To be able to access your food easily during hiking, you can put granola bars in the side or outer pockets of your backpack. Food that you might need later on during the day (e.g. peanut butter, wraps etc.) can be stored in a larger Zip Lock bag in the top part of your backpack. In this way it will be easy to reach your food, and you won't need to spend much time searching for it. It is also practical to keep your food in a dry bag. You should also bring an extra bag for garbage.

This sketch explains everything more clear:

Food for during the day (1day)

All the other trail food (in drybag)

Granola bars

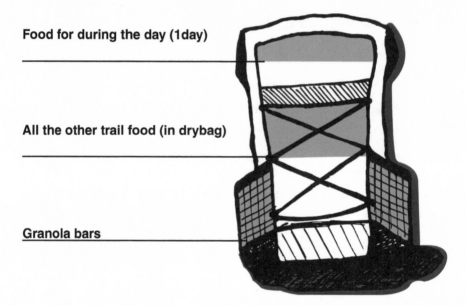

Notes:

Food parcels

On the North Island, it is not necessary to send food parcels. If you walk the South Island, you might consider sending food parcels. This will save you time during the longer sections of the hike. If you don't send food parcels, you'll need to hitch hike off trail a few times to resupply. This would give you the opportunity to take some rest or to do a side trip. Food parcels are not mandatory, but they may save you time in the long run.

Pros

• Saves time on the trail.
• No hitchhiking, which can be quite tedious, and you have to plan time to hitchhike back to the trail as well.

Cons

• If you send food parcels at the very beginning of the trail, you might not know which trail food you like/don't like, and therefore you might end up with unsuitable food.
• You have to organize and send the food parcels in the first few days (only for southbounders) because of the delivery time.The best way to do this is from Picton or Blenheim. Northbound it's less of a problem because you will have more time to adapt and see which kind of food you like. There you can send food parcels from Queenstown/Wanaka, which is after a few days of hiking.

How to send the parcels?

Food parcels can be sent from the post office. In addition to the address, always include your full name, the approximate pick-up date, and that you are a TA Hiker.

Example: JULIA MUELLER -TA HIKER- 01.12.18. In addition, be prepared to pay $5-10 for storage of the food parcel.

It is worth sending food parcels to these places

*   **Saint Arnaud** - Alpine Lodge, 75 Main Rd, St. Arnaud, RD2 Nelson 7072
*   **Boyle Village** - Boyle River Outdoor Education Centre, BROEC Private Bag 55002, Orchard Road, Christchurch, 8154
    Note: Before sending food parcels, you must contact the Outdoor Education Center. Email info@boyle.org.nz or call 03 315 7082. The address is in Christchurch, but the packages are picked up by the Outdoor Center staff and taken to Boyle Village
*   **Arthurs Pass**, DOC Visitor Center, West Coast Rd SH73, Canterbury 7654
    Note: DOC Visitor Center hours 8am-5pm.

Resupply - Overview of the complete Trail

Here is a practical overview of the individual resupply possibilities on the North and South Island.

You can find the link here:

https://www.flickr.com/photos/workingnomad/
albums/72157670624633994/with/29677223546/

Water

Where can I find water?

Fortunately in New Zealand there is plenty of water. Whether you're at a campground, in the mountains, in a hut, or in the city, you won't have to worry about water supply. If there is a section where you have to carry more water with you, it will be mentioned in the trail notes.

How much water do I take with me?

On the North Island, I always had 2 liters for the day. On the South Island, I never carried more than 1.5 liters because you can fill up quite frequently at rivers and streams.

Can I drink the water directly?

You can generally drink the water from rivers and streams, but to be on the safe side, I would recommend filtering it. At huts, you can refill water from water tanks which you can always drink from without any doubts. Signs on the tanks will indicate if you should treat or filter the water.

Water filter or tablets?

I would recommend using a water filter. The advantage is that you can drink the water immediately after filtering. In addition, you won't use chemical substances, and the filter lasts for a long time. I used the *Sawyer Mini* but would recommend the larger filter, the *Sawyer Point ONE Squeeze SP129*. It has a better flow rate, which means you can filter more water at once. Filtering water with the *Mini* is time consuming. The Sawyer filters come with a squeeze bag, but they break quickly. Therefore, I recommend taking a separate squeeze bag with you. For instance the *Platypus Platy Bottle 2L* is an excellent option. You can screw the filter directly onto the Platypus bottle as well. Water purification tablets are also available in New Zealand, but they often have a chlorine taste, and you usually need to wait 30 minutes before you can drink the water.

Hitchhiking

Resupply via Hitchhiking on the TA?

If you decide not to send food parcels, you can hitch from the following places. As mentioned earlier, this is only necessary on the South Island.

- **Saint Arnaud** - to Richmond, Nelson or Blenheim
- **Boyle Village** - to Hanmer Springs
- **Arthurs Pass** - to Christchurch or Greymouth

Generally, plan a generous amount of time for hitchhiking because sometimes, the roads are not very busy.

Hitchhiking in New Zealand

In general, hitchhiking in New Zealand is uncomplicated and safer than in other countries. Kiwis are very helpful and friendly. With a little bit of patience, you get a ride.

Tips

When hitchhiking, it is helpful to carry a sign indicating your destination. Cardboard and permanent marker can be handy to have in your pack. It is best to write your destination in bold letters on the cardboard, so that people can read it when driving by. Always stand in a place where drivers can see you early enough and where they are able to stop. Don't ever wait on a curve; it's dangerous because the drivers can't see you in time to stop until very late.

It's also advantageous to be easily recognizable, which means don't wear a cap and sunglasses, and look friendly. If you want to hitchhike out of a bigger city, it is advisable to take the bus, train, etc. first; you will have more luck hitchhiking outside of the city.

Hitch hiking alone

New Zealand is quite safe, but to avoid unnecessary risks, I recommend the following: It is always good to join up with another person and hitch-hike together. On the trail, you will meet plenty of other hikers you can travel with. If you are alone, you can always say no, even if the car has already stopped. For example, if I´m hitch hiking solo, I only ride with other women, couples, or families.

How do I get to Cape Reinga?

The easiest way is to take the bus from Auckland to Kaitaia first. This is the Intercity Bus, the costs will depend on how early you book - around 40 to 60 NZ dollars and it takes about 7 hours. If you book a few months in advance, the ticket sometimes costs only 1 NZ Dollar! You can find the link to book here: *https://www.intercity.co.nz/*

From Kaitaia, you have several options to get to Cape Reinga.

- Hitchhiking (that's what most people do), 110 kilometers, 1.5 hours by car.
- Shuttle bus, there are some providers; the details can be found in the Trail notes.

How do I get to Bluff?

There are different ways to get to Bluff.

- Flight from Auckland to Invercargill, then bus or hitchhiking.
- Flight from Christchurch to Invercargill, then bus or hitchhiking.
- Bus from Christchurch to Invercargill, then bus or hitchhiking.

Tickets for the bus can be found here *https://www.intercity.co.nz/*

Notes:

Options on the Trail

There are a few sections where you have the opportunity to bike or canoe.

Bicycle Option

- Timber trail, general information and companies with bicycle rental can be found at *https://timbertrail.co.nz/*
- Lake Tekapo to Twizel or Lake Ohau. You can get detailed information about bike rental in the Trail notes (Canterbury section, Tekapo to Lake Ohau), just call them and ask.

Options on the Trail

Canoe/Kayak Option

There are three options:

1. Cherry Grove to Wanganui (7- 8 days).
2. Whakahoro to Wanganui (5 - 6 days).
3. Whakahoro to Pipiriki (3 days) plus 1 day by bicycle to Wanganui.

It is best to organize the canoe tour from the i-Site Centre in Taumarunui. The friendly staff will give you detailed information and help you to find the right accommodation for the tour on the Whanganui River. Once you have decided what works best, you can book everything directly at the i-Site.

The only thing to keep in mind is that you can't canoe the Whanganui River on your own. There must always be at least two people, whether in a canoe or a kayak. You should meet enough other hikers to group together. If you want to be 100% sure, just create a post in the Te Araroa group so that you can find other TA hikers who want to do the Whanganui River Tour as well.

Tip for Northbounders:

You can call one of the canoe rental companies (details in the trail notes or on the Internet) and ask them if they can pick you up in Wanganui and give you a lift to Taumarunui. Most Canoe rentals have to drive this route anyway, the canoes are collected in Wanganui. Or you can take the bus from Wanganui to Ohakune. In Ohakune you can book your canoe journey through a company called Yeti Tours. They will transport you to the start point.

The terrain on the trail

Highway

If you walk on a highway, you should put your raincover on your back-pack so that you are easily visible to traffic. Always walk against the traffic, because you will be able to see oncoming traffic. If you have to take sharp turns, it is better to change to the other side of the road and walk through the curves with the traffic. Also, it's not recommended to listen to loud music on busy roads, because this will make you less aware of what's happening around you.

Mud

Walking through mud (especially in the forest) on the TA can be quite tiring. Don't bother taking your shoes off or trying to walk around, you´ll have to go through it. Sometimes you´ll be able to wash the mud off your socks and shoes in rivers or creeks.

Rivers

You can find detailed information on safe river crossing in the chapter „River crossings."

Be prepared for wet feet because of the river crossings and of walking through lots of creeks and tussock.

For instance, on the South Island my feet were wet 90% of the time, whereas on the North Island my feet were almost never. You'll get used to it quickly and it's not that uncomfortable.

Beach

You are likely to get blisters on your feet in sections that lead through sand. It's important to stop immediately and treat the area properly as soon as you notice a rubbing spot in your shoes. Also, the lighter your backpack, the fewer blisters you will have on your feet, especially on the 90 Mile

Beach.

Forest

From time to time, the trail can be difficult to follow, especially in the forest sections. On some parts of the trail you will have to climb over or under fallen tree trunks. Just keep an eye out for the orange trail markers. As long as you see them regularly you are perfectly fine.

Mountains

The highest point on the Te Araroa trail is only about 1900 metres in elevation. However, even in the high season, there might be some snow left. You should always get an up-to-date weather forecast before heading into the mountains. The condition of the trail on mountainous terrain is good, but not comparable to the hiking trails in Europe.

Meadows

In meadows and fields, you are likely to come across sheep, cows and bulls. These are harmless, but it's best to walk past slowly and at a distance. You really don't have to worry, the animals are used to humans and will avoid you.

Notes:

River Crossings

There are River Crossing courses in New Zealand, which are offered regularly. You can find information and dates under:

https://www.outdoortraining.nz/

You can find other hikers who are interested in joining a river crossing course by posting in the TA Facebook group.

General information

River crossings are a frequent discussed topic in the FB groups. You should be aware that crossing a river can be quite a challenge. There are only a few river crossings on the North Island, but on the South Island there are a lot. River water can rise within minutes. If it is raining up stream, the water level may rise without your notice. It is possible that you might have to wait for a while at the crossing due to bad weather conditions. If you have any doubts, whether you are solo or in a group, please do not cross the river at all.

For solo hiker

If you are hiking solo and feel insecure about crossing the river, you could wait and see if other people will join you the next day. If you already know in advance that you are doing a section where you have to cross a big river, you can try to group up with other hikers in advance.

Don't Cross a River When:

- The river flow is faster than walking pace.
- The water is murky and you can't see the bottom of the river.
- Larger objects are visible in the water, such as broken branches or tree trunks.

How to Cross a River:

- First you should check the best place to cross the river (no strong rapids, no big stones/objects in the water).
- Take the time to define an entry and exit point. The safest point is where the river is shallowest. Also, your exit point must always be downstream; never cross upstream.

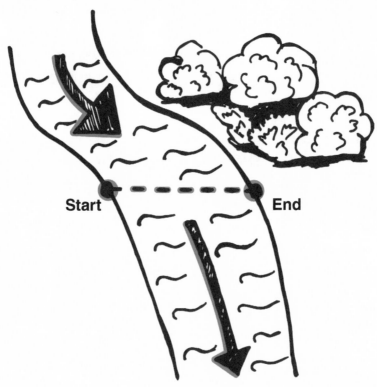

In a Group

- The more people you have, the better. You can support each other during the crossing. This increases safety.
- Open the chest strap on your backpack, loosen the shoulder straps and keep the hip belt closed.
- Line up next to each other, hold on to your neighbor's hip belt for stability, or place your hands between your neighbours back and backpack.
- The person with the most experience should be exposed to the strongest current, the weakest members of the group in the middle, and another strong person at the end in case you have to turn back.
- During the crossing, talk to each other, walk slowly, and stay close to each other.

Solo

- Use a stick or a hiking poles as support. This gives an additional support, and you always have two points of contact in the water.

Good, additional information about river safety can be found here:
https://www.mountainsafety.org.nz/resources/toolbox/river-safety/

Tip

Don't take your shoes off to cross; it's time-consuming. You can also cut your feet on sharp rocks etc. If you keep your shoes on, your feet will be well-protected during the crossing.

Rivers on the TA - Additional Info

The biggest river to cross is the Ahuriri River in the Canterbury Section. I crossed the river with three other hikers, and it was still very difficult. The current was strong, and the water went partially up to my belly button, although it's possible that the water was exceptionally high that day. If conditions are good, I would recommend trying to cross the river with several people. If you are solo, wait for other hikers or take the alternate route which leads to a bridge (about 10 km detour).

The Rakaia and Rangitata Rivers are not part of the trail. The trail notes point out in detail not to cross these rivers. However the distance between the two rivers is part of the trail. It is difficult to get there, but you can try to hitchhike. With a little bit of patience, you will get a ride. There is also a shuttle service. Information about this can be found in the trail notes (Canterbury Section, Rangitata River Hazard Zone).

Finally, the trail runs along the Deception River around Arthurs Pass. Sometimes you walk literally in the river. This section is very nice when the weather is good, especially because it offers many opportunities to swim. In bad weather this part of the TA can be very difficult and dangerous.

Notes:

Bathing

On the TA, you´ll have the opportunity to take a shower every 5 to 6 days. This might take a while to get used to it, but keep in mind that everyone else is doing the same thing. Also deodorant is rather unnecessary, because you won't smell good during a long distance hike anyway.

Clothes can be washed at campsites. In order to share the costs of washing (washing and drying cost 4 NZ dollars each), it makes sense to group together with another person. Of course underwear and socks can be washed daily by hand. To dry my hand washed clothes I always hung them on the outside of my backpack. Whether you carry soap with you or not is of course a matter of personal taste.

Foot care

Your feet will carry you 3,000 kilometers through New Zealand, so it's vital to take good care of them. Here are some tips I would like to share with you:

- The right shoes are the most important thing! If the shoes don't fit, the trail can become real torture. More information about the right shoes can be found in the next chapter (Equipment).

- Reduce your backpack weight as much as possible.

- As soon as you notice a friction, stop and treat it properly. Keep in mind that this is very important, especially in the first few days. Yes, it can be a bit annoying to stop several times and put more tape etc. on your skin, but it's worth it. The trail is not a race and your feet will be thankful for the good care.

- There are several options to avoid getting blisters. My favorite one is sheep wool! You will pass many sheep farms on the TA. Most of the time, you can see bits of wool hanging on the fences. Just collect them and put them in a small Ziploc bag. You don't have to wash the wool either, as the fat in the wool is part of how it takes the friction off the feet. If you start in Cape Reinga, it is best to get your "Hiker wool" before you begin because the trail starts with a beach. The wool can be wrapped or taped around toes.

- Taping. This can be done to prevent and treat blisters. As a precaution, simply tape any areas where you have concerns about getting blisters. For example, I often taped around my heels. You can leave the tape on your skin for a few days, even while showering. You can also wrap up single toes or the balls of your feet.

- If you already have a blister, it's best to pop it with a clean needle and let it dry out overnight. The next day put a compression pad on the blister and tape it carefully. Without the extra pad, you'll pull your skin off when you take the tape off. The best tape is the skin-colored *Leukoplast* tape. You can buy tape and compress in any pharmacy in New Zealand.

- Massage your feet with tea tree oil and some cream every day after hiking. Tea tree oil is antiseptic, and the cream moisturizes your feet. A short massage after a long day of hiking is wonderful!

- Keep your toenails short, otherwise you might lose one or two!

Notes:

Equipment

In general, the chances are very high that a few things will break and need to be replaced during your hike. It is almost impossible to walk 3,000 kilometers without breaking any piece of equipment. You should also be aware of the weight of your backpack. In the long run, you'll notice every extra kilo in your pack, even if it's just one or two. That's why you should reduce your equipment as much as possible. However, never compromise your safety. Sorting out unnecessarily gear is often a step by step process during the hike. For example, at the start of the TA, I had a base weight of 16 kilos and in the end I was able to reduce it down to 10 kilos. With good „lightweight equipment" it is definitely possible to reduce your pack weight. I personally think that the trail is more enjoyable if you don't have to carry that much with you.

Shoes

Almost all hikers on the TA use trail runners. These are basically normal sneakers, but with a bit more profile. They are lightweight and dry quickly. I think trail runners are definitely the best solution for this trail because you can walk in every kind of terrain. I wouldn't recommend using heavy hiking boots at all, as they are more useful for mountaineering.

Special insoles for your shoes may also be helpful. Also, keep in mind that your feet must have enough room, so it might be good to buy them a size bigger than normal. It's also handy to try the shoes on with your hiking socks.

The Big 4 - Save the most weight with these items.

Backpack

Besides shoes, your backpack is one of the most important pieces of equipment for the trail, so you should make sure that it fits you well. It should weigh as little as possible. Nowadays there are excellent light-weight backpacks; you won't need anything larger than 45-55 liters.

You will also need a good rain cover, preferably in a bright color, so that you are visible while walking on roads. Good backpack brands include *ÜLA* or *Hyperlight*.

I walked the whole trail with a backpack that had a base weight of 3.5 kilos, which is very heavy. If I'd had a backpack with a base weight of one kilo, I would have saved 2.5 kilos! That means I could have carried 15 bars of my favorite New Zealand chocolate (Whittaker's) with me.

Sleeping Bag

When it comes to choosing the right sleeping bag, you will have the choice between down and synthetic sleeping bags. Down sleeping bags are very light and keep you extremely warm. These sleeping bags are compact and will last for years with proper care. The disadvantage of down is that it takes a very long time to dry once it gets wet. If you should decide to buy a down sleeping bag, it makes sense to invest a little more money and get a good, long-lasting product. A dry/compression bag might be handy as well.

Synthetic fiber, on the other hand, is heavier than down, but it's no big deal if the bag gets wet. Synthetic sleeping bags are also very easy to clean.

I had a synthetic sleeping bag for many years and finally decided to switch to a down product because the characteristics are simply unbeatable. For the TA I would recommend a sleeping bag with a low temperature rating because it can get quite cold, especially on the South Island. My sleeping bag had a comfort zone of - 3 degrees, but I do freeze quickly, and everyone has a different sense of cold.

Mattress

When it comes to mattresses, there are generally two options. You can choose between an inflatable mattress or a sleeping pad. Personally, I find a mattress more comfortable, but it takes a little longer to set up because you'll need to inflate it first. I've tried the sleeping pad too, and I found it not so comfortable and occasionally chilly. It is important to check that the products have good insulation properties, and, of course, they shouldn't be too heavy.

Tent

To choose the right tent you should first decide if you want a one or a two-person tent. Then everything comes back to quality and weight. If you make a smart decision you can easily save weight without compromising quality.

The *MSR Hubba NX* (available for 1 or 2 person) is very easy to pitch and collapse; it's solid and light (1290 grams or 1500 grams), but it's not an ultralight tent. If you want to save even more weight, the best-known models are the *Zpacks duplex Ultralight* with 550 grams or the *Tarptent pro trail* with 760 grams. You need hiking poles to set up both models.

Packing list for the Trail

Here is an overview of the equipment for the trail.

Clothes

- Shoes
- Flip Flops
- Rain jacket
- Rain trousers (optional)
- Socks (wool), 2 Pairs (one for hiking the other one for sleeping)
- Underwear (3 pairs, best is wool underwear)
- 1 Long-Sleeve (wool)
- 1 Shirt oder Long-Sleeve
- Cap or hat
- Buff (neck warmer)
- Beanie
- Down jacket
- Fleece sweater (you can use the sweater or the down jacket as a pillow)
- Sport´s bra (for female hikers)
- For women: 2 Leggings, (one to hike, one to sleep)
- For men: 1 trousers (hiking) + 1 Leggings (sleeping)
- Gaiters (optional)

Toiletries

- Sun creme (high SPF)
- Tape (Leukoplast)
- Tea tree oil and small creme
- Sheep wool
- Comb
- Tooth brush
- Tooth paste
- Earplugs (if someone is snoring in a hut)
- Dental floss (you can also fix e.g. holes in shoes because dental floss is tear-resistant).
- Towel (small size)
- Sanitary products (for women)
- Nail clipper

Electronics

- Power bank
- Phone with waterproof case
- cabels to charge (phone and power bank)
- Adapter
- Head phones
- USB-stick or memory card (with trailnotes and topo maps on it), everything stored in a Ziploc bag

The big 4
- Sleeping bag
- Mattress/sleeping pad
- Tent
- Rucksack

First Aid Kit
In general, you won't need a whole package of the articles listed in the First Aid Kit, just take a few tablets, medical wipes, etc. with you.

- Pain killers (Ibuprofen)
- Imodium
- Medical wipes
- Antihistamin
- Emergency blanket

Repair Kit
- Needle and thread
- Tent repair tape
- Repair kit for mattress
- spare rope for clothes (optional)
- Safety pins (replacement for clothes pegs)

Cooking

- Cooking pot - a sponge is rather inpractical because it starts to smell bad after a while. However it´s easy to clean the pot by hand.
- Gas stove
- Spork (cobination of fork and spoon)
- Pocket knife

Miscellaneous

- Hiking poles – you can wrap duct tape around each pole, that´s very useful if you need to repair things.
- Map case, just if you want to print out the maps
- Compass
- Sun glasses
- Shovel (optional)
- E-book reader (optional)
- Torch
- 3 – 4 Drybags (for food and clothes)
- Permanent marker (for hitch hiking)
- Compression bag for sleeping bag (optional)
- Small carabiners (to attach things to your backpack, e.g. PLB, flip flops, clothes etc.)

Water

- Camel bag or water bottle
- Water filter (*Sawyer Point ONE Squeeze SP129*)
- Squeeze bottle (*Platypus 2L*)

Documents

- Passport
- Credit card
- Confirmation for travel health insurance
- Visa for New Zealand

In New Zealand

- PLB (if you already have one make sure to put it in the carry-on baggage. Otheriwse, depending on the airline company, they might take it out of your pack).
- Lighter
- Camping gas
- Batterie for torch
- Toilet paper
- Cah for camping (Honesty box)

How Do I pack my backpack correctly?

In general, it's handy to pack the backpack so that all items and food are easily accessible. Heavy equipment should be placed in the middle of the backpack, close to the centre of gravity. In addition, it is practical to have rain gear and raincover easily at hand, as the weather in New Zealand can change quickly.

For me it was extremely important that my sleeping bag and my set of spare clothes stay dry. Therefore I use a combination of dry bags (clothes, tent, food) and zip lock bags (electrical stuff, First aid kit etc.) in different sizes. This also helped me keep a good overview of what was in my backpack.

Your tent will be wet in the morning because of the humidity in New Zealand. But You can normally let it dry during the day, e.g. during your lunch break.

Storage of things that you don't need on the trail

If you plan to stay a bit longer in New Zealand after you finished the TA, or if you are already in NZ before starting the trail, you will definitely need a place where you can store your extra belongings. Quite often, you can find great people (so-called trail angels) who will offer to store your things for free.

A post in the Te Araroa Facebook group can be helpful. There is also a website, *https://trailangel.co.nz/* , where locals offer their help. You will see that there are many great and supportive people in New Zealand.

How Much Does the Trail Cost?

General

Walking the North Island is definitely more expensive than the South Island because you have to pay for camping almost every night. Additional expenses include the canoe trip on the Whanganui River, the journey to Cape Reinga, and the ferry from Wellington to Picton. The South Island is usually a bit cheaper, especially as you can almost always sleep in huts. In addition, you won't be able to spend so much extra money because you rarely walk through cities and towns.

Food is much more expensive in New Zealand than in Europe. Also, you should consider that you'll need to replace equipment at some point because 3,000 kilometers is a long way to go. I for instance needed to replace:

- 1 pair of shoes (I used 2 pairs in total)
- 1 x long-sleeve
- 3 pairs of socks
- 1 set of hiking poles
- 2 x leggings
- 1 pair of flip flops

In addition, the costs vary depending on your choice of accommodation because there's a huge difference between sleeping in hotels or hostels and campgrounds. Your expenses will vary depending on what hiking gear you already have and how long you will need to hike the trail. Then, of course, it also depends if you already have some hiking gear and how long you'll need for the trail.

Overview of Expenses

This overview is only a rough guideline and should help you understand how much money you should expect to spend. In the example, I assume that it takes 4.5 months (140 days) for the complete trail (North and South Island, without rest days). The calculation does not include flight, visa, health insurance and equipment that you bought before the trail.

Accommodation- Tent (80 days), Huts (30 days), Free Camping (15 days), Hostel (15 days)

1960 $

Food, - Trail food, snacks, coffee etc.

3960 $

Transport

350 $

Phone plan

72 $

Food parcels

90 $

Activities - Whanganui river, mountainbike rental, Queen Charlotte Trail

450 $

Miscellaneous - camping gas, medicine, batteries etc.

175 $

Equipment replacement - Shoes, T-shirt, leggins, socks etc.

547 $

7604 $

Let's go

If you've decided to do the trail, don't let anyone stop you! Always keep in mind that it's just walking, and anyone can do it. It is going to be an amazing adventure. Hiking the TA was one of the best things I have ever done. I always smile when I think back on the wonderful people I met and stunning landscape of New Zealand.

If you have any questions please feel free to contact me via my website *www.teararoaguide.de* or *www.fernwanderin.de*. I am curious about your experience on the trail and whether my guide helped you!

I wish you lots of fun and great adventures on the trail.

Cheers,
Caro